The B
CHOWDERS

Dorothy Murray

BRISTOL PUBLISHING ENTERPRISES
Hayward, California

Printed in the United States of America.

ISBN: 1-55867-289-3

Cover design: Frank J. Paredes

CHOWDER ORIGINS AND INGREDIENTS

Chowders are thick, chunky, hearty soups. Although clam chowder is the most commonly known, there are many different variations of this classic dish. The word chowder is often used to describe any thick, creamy soup with chunks of food. Even the ubiquitous clam chowder comes in a variety of textures and flavors depending on the region producing it.

Although the exact origin of chowder remains in dispute, what is certain is the importance of chowder in American cuisine. It has become a quintessential American dish, and the question of its preparation has been the subject of many heated debates. There has been such controversy in the Eastern United States over the ingredients of clam chowder that in 1939 a state legislator from Maine tried to introduce a bill to make it illegal to add tomatoes to chowder.

The word chowder probably comes from the French word 'chaudiere,' a cauldron in which fishermen made their stews fresh from the day's catch. The first chowders contained seafood, making it probable that chowder originated in a fishing community.

As with any dish, the quality of ingredients used will affect the final product. When making any kind of seafood chowder, spend extra time ensuring the freshness of the seafood. It will really pay off in the final result, as well as ensure food safety standards.

Salt pork is very common in chowder recipes; it is usually diced and sautéed until most of the fat is rendered. The drippings can be used to sauté vegetables. Salt pork is quite salty(!) so use salt sparingly in these recipes. If you're not a purist, you may use bacon instead of salt pork. A 2-inch square of salt pork is equivalent to about 3 slices of bacon. Diced and fried Canadian bacon or smoked ham are also good substitutes.

In this book, you will also find recipes for flavorful stocks (essential for a good chowder), sides and extras. Nothing completes a chowder like a tasty side of crackers or a helping of homemade croutons.

Thousands of Americans celebrate chowder in all its varieties every year in chowder festivals and competitions held across the country. Now you too can join in the culinary debate by preparing your own chowders. Learn the difference between Manhattan and New England style clam chowder—and you'll almost certainly get swept up in the national obsession.

NEW ENGLAND SEAFOOD CHOWDER BASE

Servings: 6

This is a good all-around base that is easy to prepare and goes well with any kind of seafood. Clams, halibut, crab, shrimp, salmon and lobster are all good choices; or use a combination of seafood.

32 oz. clam juice
1 cup powdered milk
1 cup flour
2 cups *Fish Stock #1*, page 6
¾ cup chopped onion

¾ cup chopped celery
1 tsp. dried parsley flakes
4 cups cooked, cubed potatoes
10–12 oz. seafood of choice
salt and pepper to taste

In a blender container or food processor workbowl, blend clam juice, powdered milk and flour until smooth. Place mixture in a large pot. Add stock, onion, celery and parsley flakes; cook, stirring continuously, over medium heat until thickened. Add potatoes, seafood, salt and pepper, and simmer for 20 minutes, or until potatoes are cooked through.

CREAMY NEW ENGLAND CHOWDER BASE

Servings: 6

This hearty chowder base is especially satisfying during winter months. Add vegetables or seafood of choice.

1/4 cup butter
1–2 cloves garlic, minced
1 cup chopped onion
4 cups cubed potatoes
2–3 cups water
2 1/2 cups half-and-half or milk
1 can (10 3/4 oz. can) cream of mushroom soup
1 can (10 3/4 oz. can) cream of chicken soup
salt and pepper to taste

In a large saucepan, melt butter; sauté garlic and onions until onions are tender. Stir in potatoes and add just enough water to cover vegetables. Cover and simmer until potatoes are tender.

In a bowl, whisk half-and-half and soups until smooth; add to saucepan. Season with salt and pepper. Heat but do not boil.

NEW ENGLAND CHOWDER BASE

This is a more traditional base for New England chowder.

3 strips bacon, diced
2–3 cups chopped onion
2 tbs. flour
4 cups warmed chicken stock
3–4 cups cubed potatoes
1/4 tsp. dried thyme

10–12 oz. clams, steamed and
   shucked
salt and pepper to taste
chopped chives or parsley for
   garnish

In a skillet, fry bacon until fat is rendered. Add onions and sauté until tender. Add flour and cook on low heat for about 2 minutes, stirring continuously. Remove from heat and slowly add chicken stock. Return to burner and add potatoes and thyme. Simmer until potatoes are cooked.

Add clams, salt and pepper. Simmer for 3 to 4 minutes; check for doneness. Garnish with chives or parsley.

FISH STOCK # 1

Makes 3 pints

Fish trimmings will consist of bones, heads and tails, which can be put into locking plastic bags and frozen until enough has accumulated. Freeze stock in little plastic containers or ice cube trays covered in plastic (to contain the smell) for future use.

2 lb. fish trimmings, washed in salt
   water
2 quarts water
2 stalks celery, chopped

1 carrot, cut in half
1 bay leaf
3 peppercorns

Place all ingredients in a deep saucepan. Cover and simmer for 45 minutes. Strain and discard trimmings, vegetables and spices.

FISH STOCK # 2

Makes about 8 cups

This is a slightly more complex stock.

6 lb. fish bones trimmings,
3 tbs. unsalted butter
2 onions, chopped
3–4 celery stalks, chopped
2 minced cloves garlic

2 finely chopped, small leeks
3–4 bay leaves
7 sprigs parsley
2 tsp. dried thyme
8½ cups water

In a large pot, melt butter over medium heat. Sauté onion, celery, garlic and leek for about 8 minutes, until vegetables soften. Add fish bones. Increase heat to high and stir continuously for 2 minutes. Add bay leaves, parsley, and thyme. Add water to cover ingredients and bring to a boil, skimming occasionally. Reduce heat and simmer for about 30 minutes, until liquid is reduced to 8 cups. Strain and discard trimmings and vegetables.

NO-MILK NEW ENGLAND CLAM CHOWDER   Servings: 6–8

If dairy is off limits, here is a variation on the New England style clam chowder.

½ lb. salt pork, diced
4 small onions, chopped
5 carrots, chopped
2 green bell peppers, chopped
10 cups water, divided

4 potatoes, cubed
2½ oz. butter clams
salt and pepper to taste
½ tsp.dried thyme

In a pot, fry salt pork until brown. Add onions, carrots and bell peppers and sauté. Add 7 cups of the water and bring to a boil; lower heat and simmer vegetables for about 30 minutes, adding potatoes to pot during last 20 minutes.

While vegetables are cooking, place clams in a pot with remaining water. Cover, bring to a boil and steam clams for 5 to 10 minutes. Discard any clams that do not open. Remove meat from shells and add to vegetables. Season with salt, pepper and thyme.

BASIC MANHATTAN CLAM CHOWDER

Servings: 6–8

To adapt this recipe to New England-style clam chowder, add half-and-half, eliminate tomatoes and float a pat of butter on top.

¼ lb. salt pork, diced
2 onions, chopped
½ cup chopped celery
2–3 tbs. flour
4 cans (6 oz. cans) canned clams,
   juice drained and reserved

1 pint peeled, chopped tomatoes
3 potatoes, cubed
salt and pepper to taste
1 pinch dried thyme for garnish
1 pinch celery seed for garnish

In a pot, fry salt pork until brown. Remove salt pork from pot and place on paper towels to drain. Sauté onion and celery in drippings for about 5 minutes. Stir in flour to make a roux. Cook, stirring continuously, for 2 to 3 minutes. Slowly add drained clam juice and tomatoes. Add potatoes, salt and pepper and bring to a slow boil. Lower heat and simmer for 30 minutes. Add clams and return salt pork. Bring to a second boil. Serve with a sprinkle of thyme and celery seed.

MICROWAVE CLAM CHOWDER

Put your microwave to good use. For clam chowder in a hurry, this is the recipe.

6 strips bacon, diced
1/2 cup chopped onion
2 potatoes, peeled and cubed
1/4 cup butter
2 tbs. flour
1/2 cup chopped celery

salt and pepper to taste
1 cup half-and-half
1/8 tsp. dried thyme leaves
2 cans (6 1/2 oz. cans) minced clams,
        juice drained and reserved

In a 3 quart casserole dish, cook bacon on high for 3 minutes. Add onion and potatoes; cover and cook on high for 8 to 10 minutes, stirring once. In a microwave-proof bowl, melt butter on high for 1 minute and stir in flour until smooth. Add to casserole dish. Add all remaining ingredients, except clams, to casserole dish. Add reserved clam juice to casserole dish. Cover and microwave on high for 6 to 8 minutes. Stir in clams and microwave, uncovered, for another 1 to 2 minutes.

SKINNY CLAM CHOWDER

Some may shy away from the rich, creamy texture of chowders. For those of us watching our waist lines, this recipe is light on fat and full of flavor.

nonstick spray
1 cup onion, chopped
1½ cups clam juice
1 large potato, cubed
salt and pepper to taste

½ bay leaf
2 cups evaporated skim milk
2 cans (6½ oz. can) clams
2 tbs. reduced fat bacon bits
parsley for garnish

Lightly spray a large saucepan with nonstick spray and sauté onions until transparent. Add clam juice, potato, salt, pepper and bay leaf. Simmer until potatoes are tender. Mash lightly. Stir in milk, clams and bacon bits. Heat for 4 to 5 more minutes; garnish with parsley.

PAUL MASSON CLAM CHOWDER

Servings: 8

This chowder is derived from a recipe developed by an Executive Chef at the Paul Masson Winery in California; it later won first prize in a chowder cook-off. Clam juice is the strained liquid of shucked clams and is a convenient substitute for fish stock.

1/2 lb. bacon, sliced
1 onion, chopped
1 green pepper, chopped
2–3 cans (6 1/2 oz. cans) minced
    clams, juice drained and
    reserved
1 bottle (8 oz. bottle) clam juice
1 jar (2 oz. jars) diced pimientos

1/2 pkg. (2 lb. pkg.) frozen potatoes
    (do not defrost)
1 qt. half-and-half
salt to taste
1 pinch cayenne pepper
instant mashed potato flakes to
    taste
milk, optional

In a large pot, sauté bacon until fat is rendered. Remove bacon and place on paper towel to drain. Remove $1/2$ of the accumulated drippings from pot and discard. Sauté onions and green peppers in remaining drippings until soft. Remove from heat.

Add drained clam juice and bottled clam juice to pot. Return to heat. Add pimientos and potatoes and simmer for about 10 minutes, or until potatoes are cooked but firm. Return bacon to pot. Add clams and half-and-half. Heat to boiling. Remove from heat and season with salt and cayenne pepper. To thicken chowder, slowly add potato flakes until you reach desired consistency. If chowder becomes too thick, thin with milk.

MEXICAN CLAM CHOWDER

Mexican clam chowder is chunky and makes a hearty meal. If you like spice, replace the can of chopped tomatoes with a can of tomatoes with jalapeño peppers.

1 tbs. olive oil
1 onion, chopped
1–2 cloves garlic
1 tbs. chili powder
6 cups chicken or vegetable broth
10–12 oz. canned baby clams,
    juice drained and reserved
3 or 4 red-skinned potatoes, cubed
one 14½ oz. can chopped tomato
    with juice

one 15 oz. can vegetarian chili
    with beans
one 10 oz. pkg. frozen peas
one 10 oz. pkg. corn
2 tbs. lime juice
1 tsp. hot sauce
1 or 2 tbs. fresh cilantro
salt and pepper to taste
chopped onions for garnish
shredded cheese for garnish

In a heavy 5 to 6 quart pot, heat olive oil and sauté onions and garlic over medium-high heat for about 5 minutes, or until onions are tender. Add chili powder and stir until aroma is released. Add broth and drained clam juice; cover and bring to a boil.

Add potatoes and simmer until tender. Stir in tomatoes, chili, peas, corn and clams, mixing well. Return to a boil, lower heat and simmer for about 15 minutes. Add lime juice, hot sauce, cilantro, salt and pepper. Serve topped with chopped onions and shredded cheese.

CLAM CHOWDER FOR A CROWD

Makes 2½ gallons

Serve this chowder at your next gathering of family or friends. It is easy to make, can be prepared ahead of time and is sure to be a crowd pleaser. Monosodium glutamate (MSG) is a popular flavor enhancer in Japanese and Chinese cooking. It is sometimes avoided by health-conscious dieters.

2–3 tbs. vegetable oil
1 lb. finely diced ham
4 cups. chopped onion, divided
2 cans (46 oz. can) clam juice
2½–3 lb. cubed potatoes
32 oz. chopped celery
2 tbs. salt
1 tbs. black pepper
2 bay leaves
½ tsp. paprika

3 cups grated carrots
one 51 oz. can clams, juice
   drained and reserved
½–¾ cup flour
3 qts. half-and-half
2 tbs. MSG (monosodium
   glutamate), optional
2 tbs. butter
chopped chives for garnish

In a large pot, heat oil and sauté ham. Add 1 cup of the onions and sauté until transparent. Add 1 can of the clam juice and potatoes. Stir in remaining onions and celery. Season with salt, pepper, bay leaves and paprika; bring to a boil and simmer until potatoes are barely tender. Add carrots and cook for 5 minutes.

In a saucepan, add reserved juice from clams and remaining can of clam juice. Whisk flour into juice and bring almost to a boil. Add half-and-half, stirring continuously until thickened. Add mixture to chowder and simmer, stirring occasionally. Add MSG if desired and adjust seasonings if necessary. Remove bay leaves and discard.

Stir in butter just before serving and garnish with chopped chives.

MUSHROOM CLAM CHOWDER

Servings: 10–12

This is another recipe that is easy on the waistline.

2–3 tbs. reduced fat margarine
1 onion, chopped
3 celery stalks with leaves,
   chopped
2 cups sliced mushrooms
one 8 oz. bottle clam juice
3 cans (6½ oz. can) clams, juice
   drained and reserved

2 cans (10¾ oz. can) reduced
   sodium, reduced fat cream of
   mushroom soup
½ cup white wine
3 cups cubed red-skinned potatoes
salt and pepper to taste

In a large pot, melt margarine. Sauté onions, celery and mushrooms for about 10 minutes. In a bowl, whisk clam juice, reserved juice from clams, soup and wine; add to pot. Add potatoes, salt and pepper. Bring to a boil, reduce heat, cover and simmer for 20 minutes. Add clams and simmer for about 10 minutes, or until potatoes are cooked through.

WILD RICE CLAM CHOWDER

This Wild Rice Clam chowder was the winner in a contest put on by the Minneapolis Tribune.

6 red-skinned potatoes, cubed
6 cups chicken broth
2 cans (6½ oz. cans) minced clams, juice drained and reserved
juice of ¼ lemon
4½ tbs. butter
1½ onions, chopped

6 oz. mushrooms, chopped
6 tbs. flour
3 bay leaves
salt and pepper to taste
1½ cups heavy cream
2½ cups cooked wild rice

In a pot, combine potatoes, chicken broth, drained clam juice and lemon juice; boil for 20 minutes. While potatoes are cooking, sauté onions and mushrooms in butter until onions are clear. Add flour and stir well to create a smooth paste. Add to potatoes. Season with bay leaves, salt and pepper. Cook for 10 minutes. Add clams, cream and wild rice. Leave to simmer slowly for 10 to 15 minutes, or until rice has cooked through.

SEAFOOD CHOWDER FOR A CROWD

This recipe is a Canadian favorite.

¹/₄ lb. butter
¹/₄ cup finely chopped onion
1 cup grated potato
¹/₂ cup grated carrot
¹/₄ cup finely chopped celery
¹/₄ cup finely chopped cabbage
³/₄ cup frozen whole kernel corn
3 qt. milk
2 tsp. white pepper

1–2 tbs. salt
6 slices bacon, diced and cooked
   crisp
¹/₂ cup diced salmon
¹/₂ cup diced haddock
6 cans (¹/₂ oz. can) minced clams
6–7 oz. crabmeat
3 cups *White Sauce,* page 21
parsley flakes for garnish

In a skillet, melt butter and sauté onion, potato, carrot, celery cabbage and corn, adding them to pan in the order listed. Remove from heat when vegetables are just tender. Place sautéed vegetables in a large soup pot. Add milk, pepper, salt, bacon, salmon, haddock, clams and crabmeat. Add *White Sauce* and cook, stirring occasionally, for about 20 minutes. Heat to about 180°, almost to boiling. Add some parsley flakes just before serving.

WHITE SAUCE
3 cups milk
6 tbs. butter
6 tbs. sifted flour

In a saucepan, scald milk, but do not boil. Add butter and stir until completely melted. Slowly incorporate flour, stirring constantly. Sauce should be a little thick but smooth. Remove from heat.

ABALONE CHOWDER

Servings: 6–8

Abalone can be purchased fresh, canned, dried or salted. Fresh abalone should smell sweet, never fishy. Choose the smaller ones, making sure they are alive (they move when touched) and refrigerate as soon as possible. They should be prepared within a day of purchase. The meat is tough and must be pounded before cooking.

3 cups chicken stock
1 bay leaf
1 tbs. dried parsley
1/4 tsp. dried thyme
1 1/2 lb. abalone, tenderized
1/4 lb. salt pork, diced

1 cup chopped onion
2 cups cubed potatoes
salt and pepper to taste
2 cups cream, or milk
1 cup white wine
minced parsley for garnish

Place chicken stock in a pot and add herbs. Place abalone in stock and simmer until it is tender enough to pierce easily with a fork. Drain abalone, reserving stock. Lightly grind abalone meat, or process in a food processor workbowl. Do not grind meat too fine.

In a pot, sauté salt pork until crisp and amber colored. Remove pork and place on a paper towel to drain. Add onion to dripping and sauté until slightly golden. Add potatoes, abalone, reserved stock, salt and pepper, and simmer until potatoes are cooked. Stir in cream and wine, and return salt pork to pot. Remove bay leaf. Garnish with minced parsley.

DUNGENESS CRAB CHOWDER

Servings: 6

Dungeness crabs range from 1 to 4 pounds. Their sweet, pink flesh perfectly complements the creamy texture of this recipe.

5–8 cups water
1–2 tbs. salt
2–3 peppercorns
3–4 tbs. vinegar, or lemon juice
one 1½ lb. Dungeness crab
4 strips bacon, diced
1 cup chopped onion
½ cup chopped celery
¼ cup chopped green bell pepper
1 tsp. minced garlic
2 tsp. chicken bouillon

4 cups water
2 cups cubed potatoes
one 12 oz. can evaporated milk
one 8½ oz. can creamed corn
one 2 oz. jar chopped pimiento
1 tsp. salt
¼ tsp. dried thyme
¼ tsp. white pepper
2 tbs. flour
¼ cup milk
2 tbs. butter

In a large pot, combine water, salt, peppercorn and vinegar. Bring water to a boil and toss in crab. Boil for 9 to 10 minutes. Drain and reserve stock. Shell crab and set meat aside.

In a large saucepan, sauté bacon until crisp. Add onion, celery, bell pepper and garlic to pan and sauté until tender. Add reserved stock, bouillon, water, potatoes, evaporated milk, corn, pimiento and seasonings. Simmer for about 15 minutes, or until potatoes are tender. Do not overcook potatoes.

In a bowl, combine flour and milk and whisk until smooth. Add to saucepan, and heat, stirring continuously, until slightly thickened. Add crab meat and heat for another 5 to 10 minutes. Add butter just before serving.

LOBSTER CHOWDER

Fresh lobsters are available year-round and should always be prepared on the day of purchase. Bacteria forms quickly in a dead lobster, which is why it's important to make sure the lobster is alive when purchasing. This recipe uses the lobster's green-colored liver (tomalley), which is considered a delicacy.

2–3 qt. water, divided
2–6 tbs. salt
2 lb. lobster
3 tbs. butter
2 tbs. cracker meal, or 2 crackers
　finely crushed

1 onion, sliced
1 qt. half-and-half, or milk
1–2 cups water
salt to taste
paprika to taste

To steam lobsters, fill a large pot ¾ full of water. Add salt: 2 tbs. salt for each quart water. Bring water to a boil and place live lobster, grasping just behind the claws, in water. Bring to a second boil, lower heat, cover and simmer for 20 to 30 minutes, or until shell turns red.

Drain lobster and cool for 5 minutes. Remove meat from lobster shell. Reserve shell and cut meat into small pieces. In a bowl, cream 2 tbs. of the butter with the lobster liver (green part) and cracker meal.

In a saucepan, combine onion and milk and scald. Remove onion and discard; add lobster liver mixture to milk.

Place lobster shell in a saucepan, add water to just cover shells and bring to a boil. Strain stock and discard shells; add stock to milk mixture. Add lobster meat and remaining butter. Season with salt and paprika. For a little spice, add a few drops of pepper sauce.

CORN AND CRAB CHOWDER

This recipe pairs corn with crab and adds a bit of bourbon.

3 cups water
1/2 tsp. salt
2 potatoes, cubed
1/4 cup diced salt pork
1/2 cup chopped onion
2 cups creamed corn
2 1/2 cups half-and-half, at room
   temperature

1/2 cup heavy cream, at room
   temperature
1/4 cup bourbon
1 pinch dried thyme
salt and pepper to taste
1 lb. cooked crabmeat
1 pinch paprika

In a heavy saucepan combine water and salt and bring to a boil. Add potatoes and cover; cook until potatoes are tender. Drain potatoes and reserve drained water. Return drained water to saucepan; bring to a boil, uncovered, over medium heat for about 5 minutes, or until slightly reduced. Remove from heat and set aside.

In a large saucepan, sauté salt pork, stirring frequently, until fat is rendered and pork is lightly browned. Remove pork with slotted spoon and place on paper towels to remove excess fat. Add onion to salt pork drippings and sauté over medium-low heat, stirring occasionally, until softened but not browned. Return salt pork to saucepan and add cooked potatoes, reserved potato water and corn. Increase heat and bring to a boil, stirring occasionally. Slowly add half-and-half and cream; heat until very hot, but do not boil. Stir in bourbon, thyme, salt and pepper.

Divide crabmeat evenly among 8 warmed soup bowls; ladle hot chowder over crabmeat. Sprinkle each serving lightly with paprika and serve immediately.

CONCH CHOWDER

Conch has a great flavor, but is extremely tough. To tenderize conch, cut into thin slices, pound each side with a heavy mallet and chop into small pieces. Or, grind using a food processor.

$\frac{1}{4}$ cup butter
$\frac{1}{4}$ cup oil
2 cups chopped onions
salt and pepper to taste
juice of 3 lemons
2 cans (28 oz. can) chopped
  tomatoes with juice
4 cups cubed potatoes

3 cups chopped carrots
2 cups chopped celery
2 cups chopped okra
2 cups water
1–2 bay leaves
3–4 drops hot pepper sauce
1$\frac{1}{2}$ cups tenderized conch

In a soup pot, heat butter and oil and sauté onions until tender. Stir in salt, pepper, and lemon juice. Add remaining ingredients except conch. Bring to a boil, lower heat and simmer until potatoes are nearly done. Add conch and simmer for 25 to 30 minutes, or until tender. Do not boil. Remove bay leaves and serve.

TROUT CHOWDER

This recipe was created by the head chef of the U.S. Weather Bureau Station at Point Barrow, Alaska.

four 10–12 inch trout
4 potatoes, cubed
2 carrots, chopped
1–2 stalks celery, chopped
2–4 cups water, divided

2 cups milk
2 tbs. flour
salt and pepper to taste
1 tbs. butter

Place trout and vegetables in a pot and add enough of the water to cover ingredients. Boil until tender. Remove trout; skin and clean fish.

In a skillet, combine trout and remaining water and bring to a slow boil. Simmer for 5 to 10 minutes. Drain fish and leave to cool. Remove bones and chop flesh into small pieces; return to pot. In a bowl, whisk milk and flour and add to vegetables. Bring to a slow boil, stirring occasionally. Add salt, pepper and butter. Simmer until reduced to desired consistency.

TUNA CHOWDER

Servings: 4

This recipe is cooked in a Dutch oven (a heavy cooking pot, usually of cast iron or enamel-on-iron, with a heavy cover). However, any heavy-bottomed pot will do.

¹/₄ cup butter
1 potato, cubed
1 onion, chopped
¹/₂ cup chopped celery
2–3 tbs. grated carrot, optional
3 tbs. flour
3 cups half-and-half

2 cans (6¹/₂ oz. can) tuna, drained
1 cup grated Monterey Jack cheese
1 tsp. salt
¹/₂ tsp. dried dill weed
¹/₂ tsp. dried thyme
¹/₂ tsp. pepper

In a large skillet or Dutch oven, melt butter and sauté vegetables until tender. Slowly stir in flour. Gradually add half-and-half. Heat, stirring constantly, until mixture starts to thicken. Add tuna, cheese and seasonings and simmer for 4 to 5 minutes.

SCALLOP CHOWDER

When purchasing scallops, they should smell sweet and fresh; the flesh should be slightly moist and pale beige or creamy pink in color.

1/4 cup butter
1 1/2 cups chopped onion
1 tsp. dried parsley
1/2 tsp. dill weed
1/2 cup flour
5 cups clam juice

2 tbs. white wine
1 bay leaf
1/2 lb. scallops
1 cup half-and-half
1/2 cup sweet corn

In a heavy pan, melt butter and sauté onions until clear. Add parsley, dill weed and flour, and stir to create a smooth paste. Cook for 2 minutes and set aside. In a pot, combine clam juice, white wine and bay leaf to make stock; bring to a boil. Add stock to onion mixture and mix well. Bring to a boil over medium heat, stirring occasionally. Reduce heat and add scallops and half-and-half. Simmer for 5 to 10 minutes. Place 2 tsp. of the corn in each soup bowl and pour chowder on top.

INNKEEPER'S MUSSEL CHOWDER

When purchasing mussels, buy ones that are closed or that shut when tapped. Fresh mussels should be stored in the refrigerator and used within a day or two.

5 lb. northwest mussels
1 cup white wine, or water
2 medium potatoes, peeled and
   cubed
2–3 cups water
1 large yellow onion, diced
1 stalk celery, diced

2 tbs. butter
one 28 oz. can tomato sauce
2 cups heavy cream
1½ tsp. dried basil
2 tsp. curry powder
salt and pepper to taste

In a pot, combine mussels and wine. Cover and steam until most of the mussels have opened. Reserve wine and set aside. Remove mussels from shells, discarding any that haven't opened.

Place potatoes in a pot and cover with water; boil until halfway cooked. Drain and set potatoes aside.

In a pot, melt butter and sauté onion and celery. Add potatoes and toss to coat with butter.

Add tomato sauce, cream and reserved wine, stirring well. Add basil, curry powder, salt and pepper. Simmer for 35 minutes, stirring frequently to prevent scorching. Add mussels; allow to simmer for 3 to 4 minutes before serving.

OYSTER CHOWDER

As with all shellfish, oysters should be purchased fresh, stored in the refrigerator and used within a day or two. If shells are slightly open, a tap or two will determine whether they are alive.

12 oz. oysters, well scrubbed
3–4 cups water, divided
1 cubed potato
1/2 cup chopped onion
1 cup broccoli florets
1/2 cup frozen corn

1/4 cup butter
1/4 cup flour
3 cups milk
1 cup vegetable or chicken broth
salt and white pepper to taste

In a pot, combine oysters with water; water should just cover shells. Cover and steam until most of the shells have opened. Remove meat from shells, discarding any oysters that haven't opened. Return meat to pot with water. Heat oysters until edges curl. Remove from heat and set aside.

36   *SEAFOOD CHOWDERS*

In a saucepan, combine potato and onion with 1 cup of the water and simmer until tender. Add broccoli and corn. Vegetables should be cooked but not limp. Drain and add vegetables to oysters.

In a pot, melt butter and stir in flour. Cook for 1 to 2 minutes, stirring continuously. Gradually add milk and broth and simmer until mixture thickens. Add mixture to oysters and vegetables; season with salt and pepper. Heat through, but do not boil.

MEXICAN OYSTER CHOWDER

This recipe adds a spicy Mexican twist to the original oyster chowder.

2 tbs. olive oil
¼ cup thinly sliced green onions
¼ cup chopped red bell pepper
¼ cup chopped celery
4 strips crisp-cooked bacon, diced
3 tbs. chopped cilantro
one 4 oz. can chopped green
   chiles, drained
1 can cream of potato soup

one 12 oz. can evaporated milk
1 cup milk
1 envelope (½ oz.) taco seasoning
2 cups corn
one 16 oz. can oysters, undrained
1 cup sour cream
4 oz. Mexican cheese spread with
   jalapeño peppers
cilantro and corn chips for garnish

In a skillet, heat oil and sauté onions, pepper and celery for about 5 minutes. Transfer to a large pot and add bacon, cilantro, chiles, soup, milk and taco seasoning. Cover and simmer for 30 minutes. Stir in corn, oysters, oyster juice and sour cream. Simmer until oysters curl. Add cheese and stir until melted. Garnish with a sprinkle of cilantro and corn chips.

BAKED FISH CHOWDER

Get creative and use your favorite fish in this recipe.

nonstick spray
4 potatoes, sliced
3 onions, chopped
1/2 cup butter
2 tsp. salt
pepper to taste
1/2 tsp. celery salt
1 bay leaf

4 whole cloves
14 tsp. dill seed
1 clove garlic, minced
2 cups boiling water
1/2 cup white wine
2 lb. cod or haddock fillets
2 cups half-and-half
snipped parsley for garnish

Lightly spray a 3-quart casserole or baking pan with nonstick spray; combine potatoes and onions and distribute globs of butter evenly on top. Add all seasonings and minced garlic. Pour water and wine over ingredients. Place fish fillets on top. Cover and bake at 375° for 1 hour. In a saucepan, heat half-and-half to scalding and add to chowder. Return to oven for 3 to 4 more minutes. Garnish with parsley.

PERUVIAN SHRIMP CHOWDER

The following recipe is a version of a national Peruvian dish. Eggs are dropped in and poached in the chowder. Alternately, a poached egg can be placed in each bowl and the chowder poured on top.

³/₄ lb. small shrimp

2–3 cups water

1 tbs. salt

1–2 tbs. vinegar

3 slices bacon, diced

¹/₄ cup chopped celery

¹/₄ cup chopped onion

3 potatoes, cubed

salt and pepper to taste

1 qt. milk

2 tbs. butter

2 tbs. flour

In a pot, combine shrimp and water. Add salt and vinegar and cover. Bring to a boil, lower heat and simmer gently for about 5 to 7 minutes, or until shrimps turn pink. Drain water and reserve. Shell and clean shrimp; remove vein that runs down back. Set shrimp aside.

In a pot, sauté bacon until crisp. Remove bacon and discard. Sauté celery and onion in drippings until soft. Add water reserved from shrimp, potatoes, salt and pepper. Cook for about 15 minutes, or until potatoes are soft. Add milk and lower heat. Simmer gently.

In a bowl, blend butter and flour together; add to pot. Add shrimp and simmer, stirring until slightly thickened. Drop eggs in chowder. Allow to simmer for 3 to 4 minutes.

SEAFOOD CHOWDER WITH SAFFRON

Just before use, grind saffron threads to a fine powder using a mortar and and pestle. Saffron is very pungent; a little will go a long way.

1/4 cup butter
2 cups chopped onion
2 cups chopped celery
1 tsp. dried thyme leaves
2 pinches powdered saffron
3 bay leaves
12 large shrimp, cooked and cleaned

1 lb. bluefish fillet, chopped
1/2 lb. sea scallops, shucked
1/4 lb. salmon fillet, chopped
2 qt. water
2 1/2 cups whipping cream or milk
salt and pepper to taste
chopped parsley for garnish

In a heavy-bottomed roaster, melt butter and sauté onion, celery, thyme, saffron and bay leaves until vegetables are soft but not brown. Add seafood and water and simmer for about 45 minutes.

Add cream, salt and pepper. Heat through, but do not boil. Remove bay leaves and garnish with parsley.

PRESIDENT KENNEDY'S FISH CHOWDER

Servings: 6

This was the recipe Mrs. Jackie Kennedy submitted when, in 1961, the Dubuque Herald Telegraph *requested President Kennedy's favorite chowder.*

one 2 lb. haddock
3 cups water
2 oz. salt pork
2 onions, sliced
4 large potatoes, diced
1 cup chopped celery

1 bay leaf, crumbled
1 tsp. salt
freshly ground pepper to taste
1 qt. milk
2 tbs. butter

In a pot, combine haddock and water and simmer for 15 minutes. Drain and reserve broth. Skin fish and remove bones; set meat aside.

In a large pot, sauté pork until crisp; remove from pot and set aside. Sauté onions in drippings. Add haddock, potato, celery, bay leaf, salt and pepper, and stir well. Add reserved broth; cover and simmer slowly for 30 minutes. Add milk and butter, and simmer for 5 more minutes. Garnish with a sprinkle of reserved salt pork.

FINNAN HADDIE CHOWDER

Named after a small fishing village near Aberdeen, Scotland, finnan haddie is partially boned, smoked haddock. It is available in some specialty food stores and seafood markets.

one 4 lb. finnan haddie
1–3 cups milk
5–6 cups *Fish Stock #1*, page 6
1/4 lb. salt pork, diced
1 lb. red-skinned potatoes, cubed
2 large onions, chopped
1 tbs. fresh thyme leaves

4 bay leaves
2 cups whipping cream
pepper to taste
3–4 hardboiled, grated eggs for
  garnish
chopped chives to garnish

Place finnan haddie in a glass dish and add milk to cover fish completely; leave to soak for 1 hour. Drain milk and discard. Cut fish into 3 pieces and place in a roaster or large skillet. Add enough fish stock to cover entire fish.

Simmer over low heat for about 5 minutes, until fish is soft enough to remove bones. Drain and reserve stock. Remove skin and bones from fish. Chop in 2- to 3-inch dice and set aside.

In a pot, sauté salt pork over low heat, stirring occasionally, for about 10 minutes. Add reserved stock, potatoes, onions, thyme and bay leaves, and simmer until potatoes are just tender; do not overcook. Add fish and cream and bring to a simmer. Season with pepper. Ladle into bowls; top each with a thin pat of butter and sprinkle with grated hardboiled egg and a pinch of chopped chives.

SEAFOOD CHOWDER WITH CREAM CHEESE

Servings: 4–6

For a little indulgence, add some cream cheese to seafood chowder. It lends a wonderful creamy texture and binds flavors for a delicious chowder.

1/4 cup butter
1/2 cup chopped onion
1/2 cup celery
1 1/2 cup milk, divided
one 8 oz. pkg. cream cheese, cubed

1 1/2 cup diced cooked potatoes
1/2 tsp. salt
pepper to taste
2 cups cooked, chopped fish of choice, or shrimp

In a saucepan, melt butter and sauté onions and celery. Over low heat, add 1/2 cup of the milk and cream cheese, and mix well. Add remaining milk, potatoes, salt, pepper and fish. Bring to a slow simmer before serving.

CHEATIN' SEAFOOD CHOWDER

This is a very easy recipe with a complex taste that is sure to impress. If using frozen lobster, meat should be thawed and drained. This chowder is excellent served with breadsticks or French bread.

one 10¾ oz. can condensed
  cream of chicken soup
one 10¾ oz. can condensed
  tomato soup
one 11¼ oz. can condensed
  green pea soup
2 cans (12 oz. can) evaporated
  milk

1 qt. water
one 10 oz. pkg. frozen, chopped
  spinach, thawed and drained
1 tsp. Old Bay seafood seasoning
½ cup dry sherry
¾ lb. frozen shrimp, thawed
¾ lb. imitation crab meat
¾ lb. frozen lobster meat, thawed

In a large pot, combine all ingredients. Heat slowly and bring to a slow simmer.

PORTUGUESE SEAFOOD CHOWDER

Servings: 8

The Portuguese often serve this seafood chowder over rice and peas.

1 tbs. olive oil
1 tbs. butter
2 cups chopped onions
1 clove garlic, minced
1 green bell pepper, chopped
1 carrot, chopped
4 tomatoes, peeled and chopped
1 cup beef stock

1/2 cup dry white wine
1/2 tsp. sugar
1/2 tsp. dried basil
1 tsp. paprika
salt and pepper to taste
2 lb. red snapper fillets, cubed
1 lb. shrimp, shelled and cleaned
parsley for garnish

In a large pan, heat olive oil and butter. Add onion and sauté until softened. Add garlic, bell pepper, carrot and tomatoes, and stir together. Add beef stock, wine, sugar, basil, paprika, salt and pepper. Bring mixture to a boil, reduce heat and simmer for 15 minutes. Return mixture to a boil. Add cubed fish and cook for about 4 minutes. Add shrimp and cook for another 2 to 3 minutes, until shrimp are pink. Garnish with parsley and serve in soup bowls over rice and peas.

HADDOCK CHOWDER

This delicious chowder is a good way of using leftover fish.

4 strips bacon, diced
1/2 cup diced green onion
3/4 cup chopped celery
2 cups chopped potatoes
1 cup chicken broth
1 tsp. dill weed
1 tsp. crushed celery seed
salt and pepper to taste

3 cups milk
3 tbs. flour
2 1/2 cups cooked, chopped haddock
one 10 oz. pkg. frozen, chopped
   spinach, thawed
one 6 1/2 oz. can minced or
   chopped clams
1 cup whipping cream

In a pot, sauté bacon until crisp. Remove from pot and place on paper towel to drain. Sauté onion and celery in drippings. Add potatoes, broth and seasonings, and bring to a boil. Reduce heat and simmer for about 20 minutes. Add milk and flour and stir well. Cook for 2 or 3 minutes, stirring constantly, until mixture starts to thicken. Add remaining ingredients and heat thoroughly, but do not boil. Serve with bacon bits.

SICILIAN SEAFOOD CHOWDER

This recipe calls for orzo, a tiny, rice-shaped pasta often used in Sicilian dishes. Orzo is commonly used as a substitute for rice.

2 oz. orzo
1–2 cups water
3 tbs. olive oil
1/2 cup chopped onion
1/2 cup chopped celery
1/2 cup chopped green bell pepper
3 cloves garlic, minced
1/2 tsp. dried basil
1/2 tsp. dried thyme
1/2 tsp. pepper

1/4 tsp. dried, ground red pepper
  flakes
1/4 tsp. dried oregano
2 1/2 cups bottled clam juice
one 15 oz. can tomato sauce
1/2 lb. sea scallops
1/2 lb. shrimp, peeled and cleaned
one 6 1/2 oz. can chopped clams,
  drained
1 tbs. chopped fresh parsley

In a saucepan, cover orzo with water and bring to a boil; cook until tender but still firm to the bite. Drain, rinse under cold water and set aside.

In a pot, heat oil and sauté onion, celery and bell pepper for 7 minutes, or until tender. Add garlic, basil, thyme, pepper, red pepper flakes and oregano and cook for 2 minutes. Add clam juice and tomato sauce and bring to a boil. Reduce heat and simmer for about 30 minutes, stirring occasionally.

When mixture has slightly thickened, add scallops and shrimp; cook for about 5 minutes, until shrimp are just pink and scallops are no longer opaque. Add orzo, clams and parsley and heat through, stirring occasionally.

BOSTON GREEK CHOWDER

Servings: 8

This Greek chowder from the Boston waterfront is known for its lack of potatoes and thickeners. The emphasis is placed on using a lot of seafood.

1/4 cup butter
1 onion, finely chopped
4 lb. clams, steamed and shucked
about 20 pieces shrimp, peeled
   and cleaned, in 1/2-inch pieces
6 oz. bay scallops, cut in 1/2-inch
   pieces
8 cups *Fish Stock #2*, page 7

4 lb. boneless haddock fillets, or
   other white fish of choice, cut
   into 1-inch pieces
1 1/2 cups evaporated milk
2 tsp. paprika
salt
unsalted butter pats for garnish

In a heavy skillet, melt butter over low heat. Add onion and sauté until tender, stirring occasionally. Add clams, shrimp and scallops. Cook, stirring occasionally, just until shrimps are pink and scallops are opaque. Remove from heat and set aside.

In a large pot, bring stock to a boil. Reduce heat; add fish and simmer for about 3 to 4 minutes, skimming surface once or twice. Add milk, paprika and salt. Stir in seafood from skillet and heat thoroughly. Ladle into bowls and garnish each bowl with a pat of butter.

DANIEL WEBSTER'S CHOWDER

Servings: 4–6

Although Daniel Webster was famous as a statesman, orator and lawyer, amongst friends he was also known for his fish chowder. Mushroom ketchup is an old recipe and not always available in supermarkets. You may be able to find it at specialty stores or by searching on the internet.

¼ lb. salt pork
4 tbs. chopped onion
1 tsp. dried thyme
1 tsp. dried summer savory
¼ tsp. freshly grated nutmeg
2–3 cloves
1 pinch. mace
1 pinch allspice
6 oz. mushroom ketchup

1 qt. port, or claret
1 qt. mashed potatoes
1½ lb. sea biscuits, crumbled
6 lb. sea bass or cod fillet, sliced
25 oysters, steamed and shucked
black pepper to taste
3–4 thin slices lemon
2–3 cups water
cayenne pepper to taste, optional

In a pot, sauté salt pork and onion. Add spices and herbs and mix well. Add ketchup and port and reduce heat. Stir in potatoes and sea biscuit and heat through. Once mixture comes to a slow simmer, add fish, oysters, pepper and lemon.

Add water and cover. Simmer slowly for about 1 hour, stirring occasionally. For a little spice, add cayenne pepper.

TURKEY AND CORN CHOWDER

Servings: 8

Put your leftover Thanksgiving turkey to good use with this recipe.

2 strips bacon
2 cups chopped onion
4 cups cubed potatoes
one 10 oz. can chicken broth
one 17 oz. can whole kernel corn,
    undrained
one 17 oz. can creamed corn,
    undrained

2 cups half-and-half
4 cups cooked and cubed turkey
1/2 tsp. salt
pepper, to taste
parsley for garnish

In a 4-quart pot, fry bacon until crisp. Remove bacon and place on paper towels to drain; crumble into bits. Reserve about 1/4 cup of drippings. Sauté onion in drippings until tender; add potatoes and broth. Bring to a boil, reduce heat, cover and simmer for about 10 minutes, or until potatoes are tender. Add corn, half-and-half, turkey, salt and pepper. Garnish with parsley and serve with crumbled bacon.

QUICK TORTILLA CHOWDER

Servings: 8–10

This is a very quick and easy chowder recipe with a Mexican twist.

one 10¾ oz. can condensed
   cream of chicken soup
one 10¾ oz. can cream of potato
   soup
one 14½ oz. can chicken broth
1½ cups milk
2 cups cooked, chopped chicken
4½ oz. sliced mushrooms

one 4 oz. can chopped green
   chiles
one 11 oz. can corn with pimiento
   bits
2–3 tbs. grated onion
4 flour tortillas, cut into ½ inch
   strips
6 oz. shredded cheddar cheese

In a bowl, whisk soups, broth and milk. Place in a pot and combine with remaining ingredients, except tortilla strips and cheese. Stir well, and bring to a boil. Add tortilla strips, reduce heat and simmer, uncovered, for 10 to 12 minutes, or until heated through. Add cheese right before serving and heat until cheese has melted.

SANTA FE CHICKEN CHOWDER

Servings: 6–8

Add a little spice to your palate with this fiery recipe. Although corn is optional, it gives the chowder a full-bodied consistency and adds to the Southwestern flavor.

3 tbs. butter, margarine or bacon grease
½ cup chopped onion
about 1½ lb. boneless chicken breasts, cubed
2 tsp. chicken bouillon, granules or cubes
1 cup hot water
¼ tsp. garlic powder
½ tsp. cumin

2 cups half-and-half
8 oz. Monterey Jack cheese, shredded
one 16 oz. can cream style corn, optional
one 4 oz. can chopped green chiles, undrained
hot pepper sauce, to taste
chopped cilantro for garnish
pimiento for garnish

In a heavy bottomed pot, melt butter and sauté onion and chicken until chicken has browned.

Dissolve bouillon in hot water and add to pot with garlic powder and cumin. Bring to a boil, reduce heat, cover and simmer for 6 to 7 minutes.

Add half-and-half, cheese, corn, chiles and hot pepper sauce. Simmer, stirring over low heat, until cheese has melted. Garnish with a pinch of cilantro and pimiento.

JULIA'S CHICKEN CHOWDER

Servings: 6

Soothe a cold with this satisfying chicken chowder.

2 tbs. butter
4 cups chopped onion
2 tbs. flour
4 cups warm chicken stock
4 cups cooked, sliced potatoes
1/4 tsp.dried thyme
1/4 tsp. dried celery salt

1 pinch dried dill weed
salt and pepper to taste
1–2 cups cooked, chopped
    chicken breast or thigh
chopped parsley or chives for
    garnish

In a pot, melt butter and sauté onions. When onions are tender, add flour and cook slowly for 2 minute, stirring continuously. Remove from heat and slowly blend in chicken stock. Add potatoes, thyme, celery salt, dill weed, salt and pepper. Simmer for 20 minutes. Add chicken just before serving and simmer for 1 to 2 minutes. Garnish with chopped parsley and chives.

CHORIZO CHOWDER

Chorizo is a seasoned pork sausage. If you are unable to find it in your supermarket, any pork sausage will do.

¼ lb. pork sausage or chorizo sausage, casing removed and cubed
2 tbs. chopped onion
3 cups milk

2 cups potato, cubed
1 bay leaf
one 8 oz. can creamed corn
salt and pepper to taste

In a saucepan, sauté sausage until cooked through and crisp. Remove sausage from pan and place on paper towels to drain. Add onion to sausage fat and cook until tender. Spoon off excess fat from pan and discard. Add milk, potatoes and bay leaf to pan. Simmer for about 20 minutes, or until potatoes are tender. Stir in corn, heat through and season with salt and pepper. Remove bay leaf before serving. Sprinkle sausage pieces over each serving.

HAM AND VEGETABLE CHOWDER

Servings: 6

This recipe is sure to become a family favorite.

1½ cups cubed potatoes
½ cup chopped onion
½ cup chopped celery
½ cup grated carrot
1 cup broccoli florets
2 chicken bouillon cubes
1½ cups water

½ cup butter, or margarine
⅓ cup flour
2 cups milk
½ tsp. salt
1 pinch pepper
½ cup cooked, cubed ham
½ cup shredded cheddar cheese

In a large pot, combine all vegetables with bouillon cubes and water. Cook for about 20 minutes, or until vegetables are just tender; do not overcook. In a saucepan, melt butter and stir in flour to make a roux. Cook, stirring continuously, for about 2 minutes. Add milk, salt and pepper. Bring to a boil and simmer, stirring occasionally, for 2 or 3 minutes. Add roux and ham to vegetables and simmer for another 10 minutes; stir in cheese and heat just until it melts.

HAM AND BEAN CHOWDER

Use your bean of choice for this recipe. All dried beans must be soaked over night before cooking.

1 cup dry beans, soaked	1 cup cubed potato
4 cups water	1 1/2 cups half-and-half
1 ham hock, about 1/2 lb.	salt and pepper to taste
1 onion, chopped	2 tbs. butter

In a pot, combine beans, water and ham hock. Cover and cook for about 1 1/2 hours, or until ham is almost fully cooked. Add onion and potato and allow to simmer for about 30 minutes.

Remove ham hock from pot and cool for 5 to 10 minutes.Cut meat from bone and chop into bite-sized pieces; return meat to pot and stir well. Add half-and-half, salt and pepper. Add butter just before serving.

POTATO CHOWDER WITH HAM

Chowder is not just an East coast preoccupation. The sweet potatoes in this recipe give this chowder a distinctly Southern flavor.

3 tbs. butter or margarine
1/2 cup chopped onion
1/2 cup chopped celery
2 cups water
2 chicken bouillon cubes
1 3/4 cups chicken broth
3 potatoes, cubed
1 sweet potato, cubed
2 cups cooked, diced ham

3–4 drops hot pepper sauce
1/2 tsp. oregano
1 pinch pepper
1/2 tsp. garlic powder
1/2 tsp. seasoned salt
2 cups milk
4 tbs. flour
parsley for garnish

In a large pot, melt butter and sauté onion and celery. Add water, bouillon cubes and chicken broth. Combine remaining ingredients except milk and flour. Bring to a boil, lower heat and simmer for 20 minutes, or until potatoes are tender.

In a bowl, whisk milk and flour and slowly add to chowder. Increase heat and simmer, stirring occasionally, for 2 to 3 minutes. Serve with snipped parsley.

BLACK-EYED PEA CHOWDER

Servings: 3–4

This recipe is from Texas and is an excellent example of how various regions have adapted chowders to incorporate local ingredients.

½ lb. smoked bacon, diced
2 cups onion
2 cups chopped celery
2 cups green pepper

1 can beef consommé
2 cans (1 lb. can) black-eyed peas
2 cans (1 lb. can) tomatoes

In a saucepan, sauté bacon with onion, celery and green pepper. When onions are tender, add beef consommé, black-eyed peas and tomatoes, and bring to a boil. Reduce heat and simmer for 35 to 40 minutes.

CHEESE CHOWDER

Servings: 7–8

A favorite of Governor Robert D. Ray, this recipe was served often across Iowa while he was governor of the state from 1968–1978.

4 tbs. butter or margarine
1 cup chopped potato
½ cup chopped carrot
½ cup chopped celery
½ cup chopped onion
½ cup chopped green pepper
3 cups chicken broth

1 dash white pepper
2 cups milk
½ cup flour
3 cups shredded sharp processed
   American cheese
1 tbs. snipped parsley

In a Dutch oven or heavy-bottomed pot, melt butter and sauté potato, carrot, celery, onion and green pepper until tender, but not brown. Add chicken broth and pepper. Cover and simmer for 30 minutes.

In a bowl, blend milk and flour and add to pot with cheese and parsley. Simmer, stirring occasionally, until thick and bubbly.

FRESH CORN CHOWDER

Servings: 6–8

Fresh cobs of corn can be refrigerated for up to a day. Strip off the husks and silk just before cooking. For roasted corn chowder, lightly butter corn and cook on a grill for a few minutes, rotating often, before scraping cobs.

6 ears fresh corn
1/4 cup chopped onion
1/2 cup water
salt to taste
1 qt. milk, divided
2 tbs. butter or margarine

1/4 tsp. pepper
3 tbs. flour
1 egg
bacon bits for garnish
paprika for garnish

Cut tips off kernels with a sharp knife and scrape cobs. In a saucepan, combine corn, onion, water and salt. Bring to a boil; reduce heat, cover saucepan and simmer, stirring occasionally, for 15 minutes, or until corn is barely done. Stir in 3 1/2 cups of the milk, butter, more salt if needed, and pepper.

In a bowl, combine flour with remaining milk and whisk until smooth. Slowly stir into saucepan mixture. Simmer until chowder reduces to a slightly thicker consistency.

In a bowl, slightly beat egg to break yolk. Slowly stir one cup of hot chowder into egg; return to saucepan and cook over low heat for 2 minutes. Garnish with bacon bits and paprika.

SUCCOTASH CHOWDER

Servings: 6

Succotash, a dish of lima beans and corn kernels, is a Southern favorite. This recipe transforms succotash into a chowder; it makes a delicious vegetarian meal.

2–3 tbs. butter
1 cup chopped onion
1 cup chopped celery
4 tbs. flour
1 qt. half-and-half
2 potatoes, cubed
2 cans (10¾ oz. can) cream of celery soup
⅓ cup chopped parsley, or 2 tbs. dried parsley flakes

1 tbs. Worcestershire sauce
3–4 dashes seasoned salt
3–4 dashes lemon pepper
1 cup sliced or grated carrots
1 can creamed corn
1 can baby lima or green beans
snipped chives for garnish

In a pot, melt butter and sauté onions and celery until tender. Add flour and stir until well blended. Slowly add half-and-half and bring to a gentle simmer.

Add potatoes, soup, parsley, Worcestershire sauce, seasoned salt and lemon pepper. Bring to a boil, reduce heat and simmer, covered, for 25 minutes, stirring occasionally.

Add carrots and simmer for another 12 minutes, or until vegetables are tender. Add corn and beans and simmer for 5 minutes. Garnish with a pinch of snipped chives.

HOMEMADE CROUTONS

Once you have tasted homemade croutons, the cardboard taste of store purchased croutons will never be satisfactory again. Any kind of bread can be used. French bread is particularly good.

½ cup melted butter	1 tbs. fennel seed
¼ cup olive oil	1 tbs. sesame seed
8 cups bite-sized bread pieces	2 tsp. dried rosemary
3 tbs. chopped fresh parsley	1 tsp. dried thyme
1 tbs. granulated garlic	1 tsp. paprika

In a bowl, combine butter and olive oil. Add bread and toss until all pieces are covered. Add remaining ingredients and mix well. On a sheet pan, arrange bread in a single layer and bake at 375° for 10 minutes, or until golden brown.

HERB OYSTER CRACKERS

Add a personal touch to the crackers you serve with your chowders.

1½ tbs. butter
¼ tsp. dried rosemary
¼ tsp. dried thyme
1½ cups oyster crackers

In a pan, melt butter. Remove from heat; add herbs and stir well. Add crackers and toss to coat. On a sheet pan, arrange crackers in a single layer and bake at 350° until golden brown.

DELUXE GARLIC TOAST

This garlic bread perfectly complements seafood chowders.

1 loaf French bread
1/4 cup butter, softened
2–3 tbs. garlic olive oil
2 cups grated Parmesan cheese
2 cups grated sharp cheddar cheese
1 tsp. paprika

Slice loaf in half. In a bowl, whip butter and oil. Spread a thin layer of garlic butter on each half of bread. Sprinkle each half with a layer of Parmesan and cheddar cheese. Sprinkle paprika on top. Cover with waxed paper, and keep in the fridge for 24 hours. To serve, place bread on pan and heat thoroughly in a hot oven. Make sure not to overcook, as bread will get too dry and crunchy. Cut into generous pieces.

BREAD BOWL

Chowder is often served in bread bowls in restaurants. Use round sour dough or Italian bread, ensuring the bread is a generous size to contain the chowder easily.

round bread of choice
1 clove garlic, peeled and cut in half
2–3 tbs. olive oil

Cut ¾-inch-thick piece from the top of the bread to make a lid. Hollow out the center of the bread. Rub insides of bread bowl with the cut side of garlic and brush with olive oil. Bake on a sheet pan at 350° for 5 to 10 minutes, or until slightly toasted.

INDEX